# Books by Dave Smith

*Poetry*

Goshawk, Antelope (1979)
Cumberland Station (1977)
The Fisherman's Whore (1974)
Mean Rufus Throw Down (1973)

*Limited Editions*

Blue Spruce (1980)
In Dark, Sudden with Light (1977)
Drunks (1975)
Bull Island (1970)

# Dream Flights

THE SETTING SUN
COURT of the SUN and STARS
PANAMA PACIFIC EXPOSITION
(SAN FRANCISCO 1915)

E 72

# Dream Flights

## Poems by Dave Smith

University of Illinois Press

Urbana · Chicago · London

Publication of this work was supported in part by a
grant from the Illinois Arts Council, a state agency

Acknowledgments are due to the editors of
the following magazines for first publication of these poems,
sometimes under different titles and in different forms;

*Atlantic Monthly:* "Wildfire"
*New England Review:* "White Beach, Black Beach: Buckroe, Virginia"; "Crab"
*New Yorker:* "Mud Holes"; "Elegy in an Abandoned Boatyard"; "The Colors of Our
  Age: Pink and Black"; "Cleaning a Fish"; "Dream Flight"
*Ploughshares:* "Breech: Birth: Dream"
*Poetry:* "Two Poems from Western America"
*Portland Review:* "Artificial Niggers"
*Prairie Schooner:* "The Pornography Box"; "The Traveling Photographer: Circa
  1880"; "Going Home: Ben's Church, Virginia"; "The Water Horse"
*Southern Poetry Review:* "Three Memories from a Southern State" (Parts 1 & 2)
*Three Rivers Poetry Journal:* "Three Memories from a Southern State" (Part 3)
*Vanderbilt Poetry Review:* "The Tire Hangs in the Woods"

Library of Congress Cataloging in Publication Data

Smith, David Jeddie, 1942-
  Dream flights.

  I. Title.
PS3569.M5173D7   811'.54   80-25029
ISBN 0-252-00862-6 (cloth)
ISBN 0-252-00863-4 (paper)

*This book is dedicated to*

David Jeddie Smith, Jr.

Lael Cornwell Smith

Mary Catharine Smith

# Contents

# Crab

*Like other crabs* Callinectes sapidus
*probably evolved from the oceans. But it is now an
estuarine organism, having found its best place in
life where river and ocean waters blend. What
primal drive, then, impels females to die in their
evolutionary cradle? Why are they not accompanied
by males, who are believed to seek out the deepest
Bay channels when their moment comes? And what
can we say of the sea runs who return, befouled and
spent, to sample briefly once more the estuarine
gardens of their youth?*
    William W. Warner, *Beautiful Swimmers:*
    *Watermen, Crabs, and the Chesapeake Bay*


I read once that when he had opened Thomas Wolfe's head,
the surgeon did not even look up,
his fingers needling and cradling
                 back the deep-hidden meat.

The books said postules or nodules, I forget exactly,
and more than once I have caught myself
in the Lazyboy, fingertips testing
                 the uneven round of my skull,

and again, then again.
                 They must have been something
gray as bubbles I dream
in the chittering crab-teeth
at the bottom of my historical place.

■

Late summer finds us ready to leave ancient Lake Bonneville,
where the Salt Lake laps the jet runway.
My son thinks of the Little League, my wife

comforts our infant daughter with a vision
of the family waiting, preparing
her for arms that will reach
among many voices
whose Virginia talk is, well,

                              funny!

■


I am seated separately with the middle child who is just
six, a stern dreamer like me. She takes time
to walk to the edge of our yard,
singing, remembering,

though she has nothing to remember yet, being six.

She will sit beside me, at the porthole, serene as a clam,
while I describe our country's true geography,
those wiggling rivers that come out in the end
where you always knew they would, her
unfathomable love storing it all,
each fact, guess, bald lie, and jittery joke.

                    I like to think about that,
things sinking in, the hand she'll hold
when my knots have finally come to something, as

we sail south.

■


The story starts in the DC-10's roar, recurrent, a dream
where a boy ratty-tatty as Huck Finn floats
as if on a tide to a secret spot.

He knows the big crab is there,
on dancing, hardly touching feet.

Yesterday one swipe with the dipnet and it was out,
caught, but he turned his back, and crabs
move quicker than jets. Now he'll try again.

■


I'm prepared to explain how this beauty is hard come by,
    and do.
The bigger a crab grows the harder to survive
that necessary shuck of the self's house.
He gets tired, sometimes gives up,
but tries to ride the current
home like a familiar dream. The sun calls him.

■


                                        I dream


a white string dangling in the marshgrass,
my chicken neck ripe.

I've come from the butcher, kind as a man can be,
who shook my small hand. I'm on my way
with a bag full.

My grandmother's sleeping in the dark house
always crackling with fried chicken.
I go in and go out, and do not see her

for the tide is turning. A kid I remember waves from
    shadows

of the Sisters of Mercy Hospital, his uniform
spanking white, glove slung on his bat.

I don't stop for him. I don't have time.

I seek out the mooring of boats and run when I see the
masts sway gently as feelers, run dizzied while bait,
string, bucket, dipnet chafe like armor.

Magnolia is white, mulberry red in this fine, soft hour.

■

In the garage, under the dried droppings of the mud
    dauber's
generations, we seek the string wound on a stick.
It waits where the walls join, crusted
by skin of moss long hardened
                        to black flecks.
We cut away the rotted part.
We stretch whatever has some life left
toward the old house where the family chatters gravely.

■

Look, make this picture for your memory of me, him, who I
    was!
Learn how doing it right means that climb out
until your face floats in the water, knees hooked
at the borrowed transom, the secret
place.
            See how I bend my neck,
letting sunburn cut deeply in, and clean salt?
We must hear no thing in the world,

4

breathing inch by inch, paying out the string,
passionately becoming, for all a crab can tell, beautiful
    swimmers.

■

Rehearsing in flight the haul of crabs, I talk her through
ways to manage the claws of fear.
                        At six, the mystery's
heart-tugging and true. Already she can see
what's felt along the taut string,
even those festering bubbles,
                        and the place

            deep in my head. It now will be
            remembered right. Loved.

■

When we come home to the family house, there will be
    gifts.
There will be painfully drawn, too small faces.
We will wear the sun's stitches and blisters,
the oxide smell of childhood.

She will not divulge where we have been all day crawling
loyal as the tide, then my boy, slumping and homesick,
will lash at her.
            Slowly she will retreat

into this story, her rehearsal of each deep color, touch and
    claw
I've planted all these long hours. Remembering,
she will inch them all through
everything year after year

going back to crab
where I lived.

Flying home

she will draw on our dream's power,
on the dark junked corner of the garage
where crabs bubble in thickets of old string,
claws waving as if to receive me at last,

the one who will pay me out all the years just as I was
when she and I were six,
burned,

at grandmother's.

## Mud Holes

Only in the heart-given lowering
of a boy's body, a man's if
a boy yet lives in him,
are they seen, and only then
within the live breath which
keeps August's serious weight
drifting over the salt marsh,
for you must go down, out,
into the unexamined field
that is all its great length
profitless, never of wheat
or least grain responsible.
From where you are, it is
a shiver of gold, cropped
hair of a child who once
walked at eye-chance under
the open window of a mother's
kitchen, walked into sun
as pale as that pie crust
she kneaded, or it is an edge
of a rug you have your chin
to, and smells of old dog
asleep, fire crackling near
in its near-blue of water.
In this squat acreage of
cordgrass owned by nothing
in the world, there is always
that scut, the ribboned trickle
left by the daydreaming tide,
and around it, on black banks,
the community of holes. They
seem made by no purposeful man,
with a mud-glazed Coke bottle
shoved in, as if to give drink to
the waiting dead in the earth,

but the mud soft as aged skin
keeps nothing of boots or beast's
bulk, only these holes. To have
come here up to your waist
in the whispering creation,
you must walk idly beyond
the garage, the bicycle by
hand painted with stolen
color, and nothing anywhere
ticks slower than this grass.
Then, there you are, as if
you had not, as you have,
taken the dust and gravel
of the home road in memory,
kicking beer cans and bird
bodies worn to thin parchment,
but as if from the other angle,
out of the sea, up the vein
in the heart of the world, all
before you the inexplicable
known that since your birth
has waited. Not to escape,
simply to be here will turn
you face down, will change you
almost to a wing, walking
air and reedtips. Then, up
close, the one bent inside
your body will seem scarcely
to breathe, no question formed
in the gliding jaw, merely
that long look down into holes
having no reason to be there,
as if a great snake had gone
out the other side of himself
without a sound. Nothing

8

is ever known of the makers
of these, nor of any owners,
nor with any skinned stick
can you cause the slightest
visible movement. If you are
here when water slowly hurls
itself back, you will see
how they take and they hold
like a bamboo flute the notes
no one has played yet, but
might, as you might be more
than you are in pouring sun,
only a shape among shapes
whose moves are as careful
as a crane's raised foot.
At night, years from this way
you have entered, you may find
your eyes effortlessly, slowly
cross the field of a ceiling,
your hand on a woman's breast,
not longing for a thing within
the world, but deep in the world
of your love, knowing at last
everything is here, hearing it
easily fill up like a hall
where the light, cricket-steps
of the dead have come to wait.
And it is not that you are held
by any pressure coming down
but by the deeps that wash up,
holy and unpredictable, your own.

*for Howard Moss*

# Elegy in an Abandoned Boatyard

*. . . mindful of the unhonored dead*
  Thomas Gray

Here they stood, hour after hour, whom the Kecoughtan
    believed
gods from another world, one pair of longjohns
each, bad-yellow, knotted with lice,
the godless bandy-legged runts
with ear bit off, or eye gouged,
a fair fight and no fault,

                              who killed and prayed
over whatever flew, squatted, or swam.

In huts hacked from mulberry, pine, and swamp cypress,
they huddled, ripe as hounds.
At cockcrow scratched, shuffled
down sucking marsh paths,
took skiffs and ferried to dead-rise scows,
twenty-footers dutifully designed and of right draft
for oysters, crabs, and croakers.
                              They were seaworthy.

According to diaries hand-scrawled, and terse court records,
our ancestors: barbarous, habitual, Virginians.

Some would not sail, came ashore, walked on the land,
kept faces clenched, lay seed and family,
moved often, and are gone. Of them
this ground says nothing.
                              Of the sea's workmen, not much,
no brass plate of honor, no monument in the square,
no square, merely the wreckage of a place.

                                                But they stood,
proud, surly, black and white
in the morning mist at the hovel of the boatwright,
some thieves, some new married, the hard arm pointed:
*Build me one like that yonder!*


                            Meaning
the gray hull I see across the cove,
bottom caved in, canting in the ashen water.

The arm was daddy's or granddaddy's, nameless as the hull,
but no need, then, for name, not to the boatwright
hunched in his shadow and bulk. He was known
to crush clams in his scarred palms,
and thus got his payment.
Our kin like as not, he built the derelicts,
snaking trees week-long with the pap of each
that stood trying to bear his countersunk eyes.


                            He gave credit to each son,
unless feud intervened in some veiled remark, in which case
spit drawled between the boots,
and took a stick into the great hand,
an awl good as any, to dig
on the earth the grave first line of a keel,


                            whose broad brow
would sometimes lift seaward, but nothing said,
as the shape buried in memory hove up
                                        and was
changed some, though God knows little enough,
the result, we suppose, of the material weaker than ever,
or creator's whim, that eye-blink,

or a young man's desire to be unlike
the drab hulls he must lie by days out, nights in.
But not too unlike as to start talk.

*Like that one yonder!*

He gave them no image to name change,
and tomorrow was only a best guess,
the sea's habitual story
leaving walls waist-high

and rotten as teeth,

leaving the stink of his silence

where the hulls riddled.
He had some kind of notion we must labor to forgive,
the fathers feared, shipping us to school in coarse linen,
the message sewn on our chest, with Bible and slate,
where the smart-sounding future was,

the world we entered

as blindly as I now have entered his place, feeling
through the back-flung gates of light
for the builder.

I sit at his charred, flood-smoothed log to learn
the lies he allowed each to invent
that he should rise up
to hack out once more
the hill of our future from planks, feeling
joy in my face as he boils pitch and makes ready
to join all. Suddenly I see

                and take up a cap
left as worthless to hang on a cypress stump,
and fit its stained round to my head.

Merely to wait where the builder heaved shards and chips
and abortive cuts to the tide's tongue-lap
is to feel the unconceived shape
pulse down the arm and into fingers
almost another self's, perfect, enough
to take up a stick
and loose the ingathered wilderness
of loon, crow, starling, and gull
who cannot believe what they see, but see it,

                            an immense shadow,
on water.
                  Stick in hand, I feel
my eyes harden
           and there it is,
                  the far wind-cradle
of the Eagle's wing, hunter now there, now
vanished. I hold my face up
to study how the air heats,
how under him builds the rising funnel,
building steadily myself, but also dreaming change

until I understand, almost, a problem: is he not harnessed,
himself, this light father
designed to sail like a minor god,
to come screeching down to the soft chicks
he will drive off, well fed,
with his lethal, callous-colored talons?

                    Our brothers float and sink,
lovely shadows, by the millions all over the earth.
Putting my back to the one bark-shorn trunk
they have left me, I pull the stick
in the dirt, remembering the long relevance of usage.

                                    The line grows

quick with light, with the answering of birds
crying out the only speech they have
for the unfinished country
that looms still,
dreamed, clearer and deeper,
out of the water that seeps,
out of the water that bore us all here.

## The Tire Hangs in the Woods

First it was the secret place where I went to dream, end
of the childhood road, deep-tracked, the dark
behind my best friend's house, blackberry
thickets of darkness, and later
where we stared, with our girls, into the sky.

Past the hedgerow and the house-stolen fields, past
the wing-shooting of crow remembered, I drive
bathed by green dashlight and the sun's
blood glinting on leaves just parted, then see

again the dead-end, the dying woods, that stillness still
ticking like throat rattle—and Jesus Christ
look at the beer cans, the traffic, even
hung on a berry vine somebody's rubber,

and wouldn't you know it that tire still hangs.

■

In the Churchland Baptist Church the hot ivy hung, smelling
of dust, all mouths lifting their black holes
like a tire I kept dreaming. Clenched
by mother and father who stank sweetly in sweat,
I sang and sang until the black ceiling
of our house seemed to bellow with storm
and the tire skulled against my eyes
in time with the great clock in the far hall.

Hanging in darkness, like genitals, it made me listen.

■

Years pass like Poe's pendulum into memory, where I see
one summer night I came to fistfight Jim Jenrett,

whose house she came to and she no more now
than a frail hand on my cheek, and I
am beer-brave and nearly wild with all
the dozen piling from cars. Jesus,
look at us in the ghost-flare of headlights,
pissing, taunting, boy-shadows all right,
and me in the tire spinning my childish words.

We pass also, and are blind, into the years like trees
that I cannot see into except to imagine Jim,
dunned by our words, as he goes out
near dawn and steps in the tire
and shies up the electric extension cord, noosed,
by the rope whose tire, burdened, ticks slowly.

■

Ghost-heart of this place, of dreams, I give you a shove
and sure enough I hear the tick and all that was
is, and a girl straightening her skirt walks
smack against you and screams. You know
who laughs, smoking in the dark, don't you?

There are no headlights now, only the arc of blackness
gathering the hung world in its gullet. Blink
and maybe he's there, his great feet jammed
halfway in the hole of your heart,
gone halfway.

■

Where do they go who once were with us on this dream
    road,
who flung themselves like seed under berry-
black nights, the faces black-clustered,

who could lean down and tell us
what love is and mercy and why now

I imagine a girl, mouth open in the sexual O, her hair
gone dull as soap-scum, the husband grunting
as his fist smacks again, the scream
not out yet, nor the promise
she could never love anyone else.

I climb in the tire, swinging like a secret in the dark
woods surrounded by the homelights of strangers.
She swore she loved me best.

■

In the church I imagined this place forever behind me
but now I sit here and try to see the road begin.
Blackberries on both sides blackly hang.
Tall trees, in blackness, lean back at me.
When will they come, the headlights washing
over me like revelation, in cars
ticking and swirling?

Once when my mother could not find me, they came here.
He said "So this is it, the place." It was dark,
or nearly, and she said I might have died.
I asked them what being dead was like.
Like being blind or flying at night.

I shove my foot at the dirt and swing in absolute black.
The whine of the rope is like a distant scream.
I think, so this is it. Really it.

*for Robert Penn Warren*

# The Pornography Box

At eighteen, the U.S. Navy eye chart
memorized, reciting what was unseen,
my father enlisted for the duration.
At nineteen he caught a casual wave
wrong off Norfolk, our home, called
Hell by sailors. The landing craft
cast him loose and burst his knee.
He lived, and wore his rigid brace
without complaint, and never in his
life showed anyone his Purple Heart.
I stumbled into that brace and more
when I climbed to our sealed attic
the year a drunk blindsided him
to death in a ditch, and me to worse.

Today I watch my ten-year-old son race
over the slick pages of *Playboy*,
ashamed I brought it home, imagining
his unasked questions have answers.
I remember the chairs I stacked
and climbed, the brace I put on
to see how it felt and, buried
deep in his sea chest, the livid
shapes shoved so far in a slit
of darkness a man could reach them
only hunched, on all fours. I clawed
through families of discharged clothes,
ornaments for Christmas, to feel
the spooky silk of webs slickly
part on my face where blood rushed.

Trussed on their wide bed, my mother lay
surviving wreckage, stitched back
beyond the secrets I knew he kept.
I shimmied through a dark hole

in the ceiling and listened to pine
rake the roof like a man's shuffle.
But he was dead and the box unlocked.
His flashlight pulsed through my body,
each glossy pose burning my eyes
that knew only air-brush innocence.
Sex rose in me like a first beard.
A woman with painted nails peeled
a foreskin, another held a man
kingly rigid at her tongue's tip.
I could not catch my breath.

I blinked at one spread on a table covered
by lace grandmotherly clean and white.
Here might have been service for tea,
dainty cups, bread, a butter dish,
except she was in their place, clearly
young in middy suit. Behind her a vase
of daisies loomed, the parlor wall
held *Home, Sweet Home* in needlepoint,
and curtains were luminous at a window.
I remember the eyes, direct and flat,
as if she had died. Girlish stockings
knuckled at her knees, her plain skirt
neatly rolled. The man, in Victorian
suit, cradled her calves in furred hands,
and looked at the window, placid as
a navigator. He cut her like a knife.

After school, at night, weekend afternoons,
I raced to see them do it, legs cramped
in that freezing slot of darkness, gone
wobbly as a sailor into the country.
I came and went in the black tube,
ashamed, rooting like a hog to see.

In one sequence a black man held a pool
cue to a white woman, a black woman
held in both hands white and black balls.
The uniforms of sailors were scattered,
wadded everywhere I looked. I smelled
the mothballs from my father's chest
when late at night I woke to vomit
and stare at a clock's one-eyed glow.

How long does it go on, the throbbing dream,
waking obsessed with a hole in the air?
In Norfolk, from loaded cars, we spilled
at sailors passing alleys, asking where
we'd find some girls, beer, a good time.
All answers were sucker-punched. *Bye-bye,*
*Seafood*, we screamed, then headed down
toward the Gaiety Theater and whores
bright as moths. We spit at mothers who
yelled *Fuck you, kid!* They never would.
The secrets of our fathers, we cruised
the hopeless streets blank as razors,
remembering nothing but naked images
whose neon flared like pus. Seeing now
my son bent to see I imagine at last

my father climbing before me in blackness,
with the tiny light a man carries, bent
on pained knees where I will kneel also
at nameless images we each live to love
and fear. One is a young Spanish dancer
whose crinolines flare out around her
hidden rose. Another cooks in high heels.
Among these are angels, blonde sisters,
classmates suddenly gone from our towns,
one on a patio reclined, her long leg

crooked in invitation. She does not hide
the shorter leg. Each grins and burns
into our memory, speaking in shy whispers,
who are born to teach us violations.
At eighteen what fathers teach is wrong,
for the world is wrong, and only women
know why, their eyes dark and flat.

It isn't eyes that sons remember, blinded
by what never lies or leaves, but
sun's glint on that raw breast, that
thigh where face should not be but is,
and is the curve of the world's flesh
radiant in its rottenness, the secret
that leaves, finally apart and other,
all who walk on the earth. In memory
I see how each breast, each leg, each
face hissed our shame. By accident
I became the boy-father of the house,
owner of obscenities and a family
of creeps who fingered me as one.
What else is the world but a box,
false-bottomed, where the ugly truths
wait sailing in the skins of ancestors?

Escaping them at last I left for college.
But first climbed to what he left me,
carted that box and brace to grave,
and spilled those mild faces down
under the looming Baptist spire.
I spread gasoline where he lay, then
with his Navy Zippo snapped it off.
Quick bodies coiled and flamed, ash
flecks disappearing in sun forever.
I gouged the remains in a trench

of churchly dirt, tried once to spit,
then turned in the dark to catch a bus.
His pea-coat was black as the sea
at midnight but I took it and wore it,
sweating against the cold to come.

Women smiled at me as if I'd been flush
with cash from months at sea. *Welcome,
Swabby*, one said, *You can sit here.*
I was free, I thought, discharged from
Hell into the world that, for Christ's
sake, waited. I left home in a wink.
And would not go back at Christmas,
being after all busy, being holed up
with the nameless girl, the long blade
of her body even now slicing memory,
that darling who took my coat. But
by Easter was ready, went. House sold,
mother gone, maybe married, maybe Florida,
they said. I wandered in a cold sea-wind,
almost on shore leave, until I came
cast up where my father lay. Posters

of the nailed Jesus littered the grass,
announcing our inexplicable life. I saw
the crones kneeled there in sunbursts,
faceless, soft, as if to serve the sun
dying in the background. I shivered,
then rose up, hearing traffic hiss,
and walked until I found the old road.
I wished I had our goddamn stolen coat.
Boys yelled at me, but no one stopped.
Freed, I was myself. Who understands?
I walked hours in hard places, into night,
my first beard tingling, dreaming what

fathers know. I came to a seedy house.
Among sailors I, a man, heard the siren
call us forward to sit with the darkness
under reels of lighted, loving women
in the theater called Art's House.
At love's edge, braced, we were nineteen.

So we went in.

## The Colors of Our Age: Pink and Black

That year the war went on, nameless, somewhere,
but I felt no war in my heart,
not even the shotgun's ba-bam
at the brown blur of quail.
I abandoned brothers and fathers,
the slow march through marsh
and soybean nap where
at field's end the black shacks
noiselessly squatted under strings
of smoke. I wore flags of pink:
shirts, cuff links, belt, stitching.
Black pants noosed my ankles
into scuffed buck shoes.
I whistled Be-Bop-a-Lula
below a hat like Gene Vincent's.
My uniform for the light, and girls.

Or one girl, anyway, whose name I licked
like candy, for it was deliciously
pink as her sweater. Celia,
slow, drawling, and honey-haired,
whose lips hold in the deep mind
our malignant innocence, joy,
and the white scar of being.
Among my children, on the first
of October, I sit for supper,
feet bare, tongue numb with smoke,
to help them sort out my history's
hysterical photographs. In pink
hands they take us up, fearless,
as we are funny and otherworldly.

Just beyond our sill two late hummingbirds,
black and white, fight for the feeder's
red, time-stalled one drop.

They dart in, drink, are gone,
and small hands part before me
an age of look-alikes, images
in time like a truce-wall
I stare over. The hot, warping
smell of concrete comes, fear
bitter as tear gas rakes
a public parking lot. Midtown
Shopping Center, Portsmouth, Va.,
the *Life* caption says, ink
faded only slightly, paper yellowing.

Everyone is here, centered, in horror
like Lee Oswald's stunned Ranger.
A 1958 Ford Victoria, finned,
top down and furred dice hung,
seems ready to leap in the background.
The black teenager, no name given,
glares at the lens in distraction.
Half-crouched, he shows no teeth,
is shirtless, finely muscled,
his arms extended like wings.
White sneakers with red stars
make him pigeon-toed, alert.
His fingers spread by his thighs
like Wilt Chamberlain trying
to know what moves and not look.

Three girls lean behind him, *Norcom H.S.*
stenciled on one who wears a circle
pin, another a ring and chain.
Their soft chocolate faces appear
glazed, cheeks like Almond Joys.
They face the other side, white,
reared the opposite direction,

barbered heads, ears, necks.
In between, a new shiny hammer
towers like an icon lifted
to its highest trajectory.
A Klan ring sinks into flesh,
third finger, left hand,
cuddling the hammer handle.
This man's shirt is white, soiled,
eagle-shaped, and voluminous. Collar up.

Each detail enters my eye like grit
from long nights without sleep.
I might have been this man, risen,
a small-town hero gone gimpy
with hatred of anyone's black eyes.
I watch the hummingbirds feint
and watch my children dismiss them,
focusing hammer and then a woman
tattooed under the man's scarred
and hairless forearm. The scroll
beneath the woman says *Freedom*.
Above her head, in dark letters
shaped like a school name on
my son's team jacket: *Seoul, 1954*.
When our youngest asks, I try
to answer: A soldier, a war . . .
"Was that black man the enemy?"

I watch the feeder's tiny eye-round
drop, perfect as a breast
under the sweater of a girl
I saw go down, scuttling
like a crab, low, hands no use
against whatever had come to beat
into her silky black curls.

Her eyes were like quick birds
when the hammer nailed
her boyfriend's skull. Sick,
she flew against Pennys' wall,
our hands trying to slap her sane.
In the Smarte Shop, acidly,
the mannequins smiled
in disbelief. Then I was
yanked from the light, a door

opened. I fell, as in memory I fall
to a time before that time.
Celia and I had gone to a field,
blanket spread, church done,
no one to see, no one expected.
But the black shack door opened,
the man who'd been wordless,
always, spoke, his words intimate
as a brother's, but banging out.
He grinned, he laughed, he wouldn't
stop. I damned his lippy face
but too late. He wiggled
his way inside my head.
He looked out, kept looking
from car window, school mirror,
from face black and tongue
pink as the clothes we wore.

Often enough Celia shrieked for joy,
no place too strange or obscene
for her, a child of the south,
manic for the black inside.
When he fell, she squeezed
my hand and more, her lips came
fragrant at my ear. I see them

near my face, past the hammer.
But what do they say? Why, now,
do I feel the insuck of breath
as I begin to run—and from her?
Children, I lived there and wish
I could tell you this is only
a moment fading and long past.

But in Richmond, Charlotte, God knows
where else, by the ninth green,
at the end of a flagstone pathway
under pine shadow, a Buick waits
and I wait, heart hammering,
bearing the done and the undone,
unforgiven, wondering in what
year, in what terrible hour,
the summons will at last come.
That elegant card in the hand
below the seamless, sealed face—
when it calls whoever I am
will I stand for once and not run?
Or be whistled back, what I was, hers?

In Utah, supper waiting, I watch my son
slip off, jacketed, time, place,
ancestors of no consequence to him,
no more than pictures a man carries
(unless a dunk-shot inscribed).
For him, we are the irrelevance of age.
Who, then, will tell him of wars,
of faces that gather in his face
like shadows? For Christ's sake
look, I call to him, or you will
have to wait, somewhere, with us.
There I am, nearest the stranger

whose hammer moves quicker
than the Lord's own hand. I am
only seventeen. I don't smoke.
That's my friend Celia, kissing me.
We don't know what we're doing.
We're wearing pink and black.
She's dead now, I think.

# White Beach, Black Beach: Buckroe, Virginia

She could not come here, among these cruising
sons, among the gray gape-mouths
that pass with the old songs
spilled into the easy air.
I watch them relentlessly look
for the girl whose grin
bleeds in their taillights.
Being black she could not
come here that summer, but did,
and sings near me from wrecks
resurrected to glide under
the Buckroe Pavilion's lights.
Child-bearing horses gallop here
and a calliope's nightmare pumps on.

■

Obsessive as the sea, she slipped past the cop.
Tonight I am washed back to our common
ground, through the black shacks
along the dead's road, and I look
for love's ageless child,
Celia, the Queen Street stepper,
beautiful mother of moonlight.
Once, years ago, I saw the brute
blue arm reach out and rip free
her brown breast that light made
finely gold, and white faces
sang *Nigger!* Glass-bright, yet
as glass, brittle, she broke
through a line like this one, passing.

■

For hours they wheel, the black line in the light
scattered from horses that pump
without expression. Some drop out
to lie by bulkheads in twos
and some are saddled in back seats.
In the dark almost I see them
gone speechless as the dead,
spent in the world's grit.
She trembles there, nameless.
It is night and night's business
is under way, and she has come
ghostly where once I saw her hang
above the seawall, stringing spit
down on my girl's wide screaming face.

■

*Nigger!* we screamed, but, ghost-quick, she
lost us. I remember that wall,
those who rose buck-assed from love
of a night's hunt, and I find
                              myself twenty
years later still dreaming
we roared toward Phoebus and words
I hear hissed in the night, half-
howled like pieces of song. They
nick me like small knives
she could not escape, stuttering
Celia, Celia under the moon.
Down Queen Street we ran her
and caught her and put her under the pines.

■

Who does a man beg for his life when song
comes heart-drumming and a name
shakes back the sea inside?
We lay her down on the bitter bed
of needles, who rose flat-browed.
I went in the world, cruising,
and scattered myself in words
but could not hide and heard
her call, as those now hear
the silence and the gull-screech.
We come Celia, we are pitched
among the undying as if hope
might come here and step out
free, dancing, true, and our own.

■

I sit and watch them pass through sea-whine
and star-trickle. Their faces go
around dappled and I think
of sleet spitting in D.C.
where my name once was
called. It was you, speaking
from a slit in the soft night,
dazzling and golden, drawing me down.
But I ran, I hid out in Utah, not
expecting to come round a corner
where your breath needled the air.
She's long dead, I thought, a man's
got a right to believe that at least?

■

Why won't you stay in a stinking room I remember
filled with the cruiser's blue light?

Cops came, one black, one white,
batons swinging, badges like moons,
spit-shined boots on stairs like time.
Her name? Celia, the old one, back
again, cleaned me, I said, and what about
the law? Somebody has to find her.
Ur-white grinned, *Yeah, so what, craphead?*
Well, she looked near dead, only. . . .
*Only?* The black one now, giggling,
baton in my chest,
               *This Niggertown,*
*boy. She gone, and you better run.*

■

She could not come here, I think, running
in my head where the calliope pumps
and the thousands of needles
of light leap into faces
that pass where I sit, waiting.
If only I could hear the songs
each follows I think I might know,
unspeakable nightmare of love,
where you are, what you want.
These are my brothers. We summon
you sweet ghostface, glassbody,
yourself, lifewind, shadow,
keeper and Queen of night's business.
We wait like children to rise up with you.

## Artificial Niggers

*How do you expect me to know anything when you don't tell me right.*
  Flannery O'Connor

We're gathered behind my grandparents'
goldfish pond, two boys flanking
the smaller girl. She's gray,
fidgeting as the Kodak snaps.
Her hand, making a fist, rises
as if about to strike one of us.
He is black and I am white.
We are frozen in this moment
of our famous Southern grins.

■

Once each year I go down into dust
and pull these photographs out.
Among children I watch
how the images gather themselves
into the history of our kind.
For hours we are buried,
inventing the ground, the air,
the silence that cannot speak
except in the small human voice,
never well enough heard,
singing out of the head's light
and dark memory of its place.
That water you see is the black James,
the land is Virginia, our green dream.

■

Before the three of us, in foreground,
the little pool, maybe six feet
across, bears the sun's ripple
straight as a good rope.
Our dead built it to keep
tame fish outside but near.
Note how lilies lean, tall,
yet stooped. They will break
rocks with roots black and deep.

■

We weren't allowed to play with goldfish
or lilies, but I stood over them
on that bridge long as a boy
and saw the artificial nigger
loom at the pond's heart.
His lantern cast a shadow
like time toward the southern
edge of the frame he stares from.

■

My mother snapped these "cute" shots
from the dark house. She called
but I would not leave my friends.
We stood in the red dusk, crabs
we caught that day hissing
from a basket behind us.
Claws locked in a fearful
chain, some smothered,
some ripped themselves apart.

■

The basket makes a dark sort of moon.
Our gray girl waits, eyes wide
over the head and red hat
of the artificial nigger.
Wind and years of grins
chipped his face to plaster.
He seems to look for himself inside.

Mother's next shot, through a window,
catches all of us bent over,
faces in the basket, bottoms
stained with local mud.
Legs and arms we are fused
by the camera, an odd growth
of the unseen crabs. Shadows
stretch thin. Soon we will divide.

■

But not before the incident singing
wordless as a sting in my head.
This print is blurred. Two boys
and one nigger locked, each
pushing at the other. Then,
amazed, on that bridge,
we look into the headless
figure. A slight smoke
grayly spirals between us.
The red-cap sinks invisibly.
Wasps by the hundreds are rising.

Next, the basket is tipped on its side.
The crabs run and hide. I lie
by the pond-stones, face down.

Dots or speckles cover my shirt,
my hands, my exposed neck.

The black boy, accused, has fled.
Our girl, centered, holds me
down, her fist in mid-air.
Her smooth chest shines
except for some tiny knots.
Her face is wizened, dark,
and it screams.

■

I was then near school, the fall coming,
and I lay in bed as storm gathered.
My room went black, then white
as leaves clawed and tore loose.
Half-dreaming, I heard "Niggers"—
and mother somewhere said
this place had gone to hell,
our father at war, we must
run or lie down and be buried.
Now I wake in another country,
remembering that lilied ground.

■

We look at the pictures as if they were
dreams running. In one a black girl
sits on the steps of our house.
We have gone back. She waits
for someone to let her inside.
I took her picture but can't
find it among so many. How

could you live in my house
and me in yours, she asked.
It was hot and quiet, the air
smelled of rotting crabs.
She took us to see the pond
where no fish swam. Sometimes,
she said, I dream they are
all in the air, me too,
just going around, black and white.

*for Primus St. John*

## Three Memories from a Southern State

### (With White Hair, They Come)

And are always suddenly there, the knock on glass
polite, formal, a man retired, teeth gold inlay.
Three raps, in the old manner. Stiff, courteous,

the pink flesh, wide-pored, stands in the porch shade
as it did, doubtless, for her who waited on staircase
to spiral down slowly. The black coat's threads

hang under the coiling white hair and a light grease
of sweat lies on the lip. The cane shuffles backward.
He recalls no name, says: "Sir, could you call please—

for someone is expected." That moment again, awkward
and familiar, his red, mad, extended palm offering
its delusion. Forced to it, you repeat, "Sir, no card

lies in your hand. No one waits. There is nothing
to be done." And him, "Sir, is she under the willow?"
Trembling now, his white hair loose. The ring?

Someone was expected, there had been a ring and "Oh, you
see there was a misunderstanding. . . ." And here
the hand falters, retreats, the sun through magnolia

lays down a sizzling tunnel and he passes out where
in he came, in dust dazed, and his leg, lame,
audibly drags like time. He returns every summer,

lingering like a scent at dusk in the yard. Tenant,
like him, you will forget the sun, the dark,
but the last time you were loved always asks you in.

## (Young Woman, Your Name Is Known)

Or else he does not rise from the wickered rocker
in which, in this memory, the hard eyes
glitter and pour forth in passion, as if a river

seen once is always seen, as if yours are her thighs
gone nakedly long in the sun. That first
chance of love leaps back to his breath and cries,

for your skirt is discreetly stained. Sometimes his hurt
glance follows you down the street,
and the light glows on him hot as youth or art.

If he should speak now? But he never quite does that.
In this memory it is also near dusk.
He is your tenant, your ancestor, an edge of fate

where you garden in cool dirt. Unearthing rust,
spoons blackened, some silver, you pat
your hair as she must have, the sweat on your breasts

tickling a little, then you listen. Where he sits
most days the awning is curled in tight.
What makes that rocker rock when there is no wind?

Dammit he's gone again, calling Celia, who is dead
or long gone, and not you, whoever she may be,
though he imagines you are her and asks you to bed.

Maybe he's near, like a child, saw something fleet,
a bird, say, and has gone leaving that murmur
of absence you've suddenly noticed. Or it might be

he's watching you, has been, from a stand of pine where,
white-haired, sick, he whimpers "Celia,
oh, Celia." Or hides and is trying to comb his hair.

Because you are a woman whose heart was right-raised,
you rise and go seek him out, who knows
how a lady takes time. Go then, but scarcely in haste.


## (Azaleas)

Such flowers have grown long in Virginia, perhaps
elsewhere. No one picks them except icy March.
The month that there is always the sea and salt

and wave-wide horizons and the scented bitter season
she's learned to fear. And today is nail-sudden
on her white parlor wall where a whiter absence is.

She can see, almost, the neap tide and far bells ring.
She recalls how little she knew of a man
loved in his madness, without pride. Her life is long,

is sitting in this room, ash-acrid, and counting failures
that are only the heart oozing like firestones,
her window wind-raked with first buds of azaleas.

Bits of paper tremble, some knickknacks of history
made for children of neighbors, of torn news,
but suddenly she stiffens for knock at door, as if he—

and remembers oiled slate hauled from County Fluvana:
her father's bride-gift, dark stones, and wicker
chairs for summer. How light danced on that veranda

when she was swept up, comically, and scrubbed in
   whiskers!
Footsteps sound on slate up to the door.
Afraid, she leans far forward, the steps disappear.

If now they should come again, his steps and his knock
blunt on opaque glass, oh, azaleas must litter
the hard ground with small beauties, and a black

pain come at the heart like the nail that surprises
with its sharp shiny thrust out of the wall. She
whispers the name of one whose picture hung in whiteness

before the world seemed only salted nights and debris.
Her fingers are old. He did not return
from whatever war he had attended and now she,

who understood nothing of blooded azaleas or tide's urge,
mountain-born, sits and is rootless and hopes
for something as yet unimagined, or ever remembered.

The children will come soon. They'll knock on her door.
They don't know her name, but he did. He did!
And what does this paper mean, like hair, on the floor?

## Cleaning a Fish

In her hand the knife, brisk, brilliant as moon-claw,
shaves the flesh. It grazes the white
belly just over the heart.
Underneath, the coiled fingers
are cradling a soft flesh
as if it were the jowls of the aged

man propped for a while on the bench in the park.
The head is not severed, the eyes not out.
Blue, they appear to flash odd ways
where a tree makes a live shadow.
Mostly the eyes are dead.
Nothing is in them

except the intense blue of sky the tree allows.
There is no conspiring of nerves,
no least event recalled
by a limb's high arching,
or even a girl's ascension
from a forgotten distance of water.

But there is something as she lifts the meat.
It is enough to draw down her gaze.
Now her arm rises against
yellow hair fallen
white in a childish face.
She is still as a leaf barely clinging.

I come to her like a cat in the stunned grass
and touch her to see the startled
upthrusted gleam of her face.
At brow and each cheek
like gathered beads of mist
scales leap with the sun, and are dead.

No word passes between us, but something electric
as a flash of steel makes her
cry out just once. Squatting
at the yard's edge, she
sings beyond any thought.
Her knife flies as lethal as love
and cuts quickly in like a hurried kiss.

## The Water Horse

We called it love's house and it was plain
by that creek where the tidal
changes were ordinary,

though once, Celia, we heard the cry there
of a beast's looming,
and did not know what had happened.

The cry comes
keening still out of the water-buried
acres of distance when I touch you.

But sometimes I wake in memory's
half-sight in the dark room of fear, and all
is
    vanished.

■

        Nightlong,

before the twining of our bodies had ended,
we heard the mares drumming the earth
along the frailest spirit of fence.

The stallion far off kept himself
saddled in mist, head-down in a field
he commanded alone. We heard how they called him.

Hoof-strikings knocked late at the edges of our sleep.

■

like the image of your face
in my memory, and I saw at once

a house we could live in endlessly,
and the ordinary redemption that is passion.

■

Hoof-striker,

I remember that dawn
when wide water fell down.
Many mares were lining the shore,

but one stood a little way off, waiting.
I saw how you went in.
Together two rose,
silted and shaggy, glistening.

All followed and went into the field
and there ate the misted grass
without fear, having seen

the ordinary turning of water
she commanded, you obeyed,
as if nothing had changed,

as if the world were only a place
always about to vanish, as it is
without the one summoning song of love.

## The Traveling Photographer: Circa 1880

Everything about him must be conjectured, his life
whatever a man's life is, succession of moments
under pine, catalpa, sedge, his sour
shirts, habitual horse, creaking wagon.

He takes no portraits of himself, on principle.
Yet, lying dreamless in the hot night, knows
it is all there, in plates
stacked, a joke no one learns the end of.

He laughs, and wind in the harness bell laughs.
Where, how did this life begin?
The plopping sound of the mare
makes him wish he could capture the night.

So much lost in black. He smells himself,
the heaving desert, and oddly
a wedge of butterscotch cake.
His mother, serving him, had laughed.
*Son, go far.* Dying.

Yes, *far.* The laugh, now,
burrs in his throat, but he remains
hungry, salivating at the ebb of his fire.

Closing his eyes, eyelids develop a cargo
of images (it is all there), the longing,
corn cakes, people, grubby people, their towns,
bluebonnet somewhere, stream, a snake weaving dust,
his wheels crossed it, the plate all
the evidence he was there.

Each thing is itself always, arcane
in the wagon, a junction without voice, theory, or
connection except the chuckhole's incessant clink-clink.

So little in all the world, monstrous
stars like a blacksmith's steel burning back the hoop
of his out-of-rounds wheels. The night trembles
like mountain water, aching his teeth.

Well, he will die soon enough.
He tries to remember an orchard at Shiloh,
sees instead the last plates stacked, is
nevertheless aware

his belly, too, prints the fishbone of his back.

■

Cat-squall, wolves, red-eye have been companions.
From the fire and from the glassy darkness
they leap like old friends. He is
somewhere west of Denver, mountains
black that had been green as fresh buffalo chips.

In dust before the trading post, patting his horse,
he had been ready to move on, had taken
all day two plates, bartering.
The whore was not worth it.
The minister who repaired cabinets
fixed his wagon to shut as it ought to.

At his elbow the child's hand, the laboring breath.

■

They were waiting, still in the usual way.
He could not tell them from a thousand others scattered,
cinders of a prairie fire.

Father and mother centered, grandfather, sleeve pinned up,
children like stairs, too many.
Seat the smallest in the dirt, let them
have legs crossed.

Dead in the middle, in tiny coffin, the laced burden
upright against the sod door. Stitching,
fine red and green thread blossoms
on its tiny nightgown.

Color won't show, nor hours of work nor
the idle chatter before powder's explosions.
How did it happen? Name and age of the child? Well, God's

will be done. Wait for the wind
hotly swirling, and always long for a quick shot
of whiskey, for Christ's sake.
The nightgown had blown up, her flesh all sunk, sallow,
backbone, surely, clear as a fish in shale.
Made two more plates.

Hours riding into dusk toward fire-flare and night,
he spits what flew under his hood,
spits, but it is still there.

His father, the circuit rider, had condemned him
for those "damn pitchers" and burst himself
in clots on his mother's pillow.
Smoke from the campfire wavers like a face.

■

Had he had some kind of calling, a mission? What?
Night lowers itself at him again,
red-eye, and the eerie blue of full moon.

At the stream's place, his image wobbles up at him.
The mare now and again lifts
its peaceable muzzle
to whicker whatever it whickers.

Things happen, things are. That's all.
Who has moved in the world more than he has,
gone farther, to know less?

Sometimes with his face splashed clean, flat on his back
between the stacked rows of glass plates,
the faces, unlost, try to speak.
He listens

until sleep comes, or dawn.
Sometimes their stories transform his own life,
strangers, nameless, become his father, his mother,
offering him children he calls Amelia and Darce.

Night-long they wheeze, electric as rattlesnake rattle.
Always with the first cluck to his horse
they are only themselves,
slabs of glass clinking behind him.

He has tried to be himself with poor luck.

■

Months into the wilderness, wheels busted again, fixed
    again,
pain like a broken tooth comes
in the middle of his chest.

Waking in dead heat, his shop is cottonwood shade.
Late afternoon, the last plates prepared,
what does it matter?
Why hurry to have it all completed?

Works steadily, feeling fat, sore. Is it an illusion?

Held up to the sun, the glacial doll rivets him,
her eyes open, black holes gone red
as star-burn or wolves. Tilts it, then
again, and yes they had her
off-center, goddammit.

Sits down plop on the baked dirt, and stares. Stares,
then hurls the plate to shatter on dung-colored rocks.

"Longinus, we made mistakes but we tried."
The horse, at its name, blusters
head-down in witchy green.

■

The artist wakes dry-mouthed, unaware he had fallen asleep.
In late, brilliant sun, he lifts
the second plate close to his brow.
Head and body, he is rock-cradled.

The father, long-armed as an ape taken in Kansas City,
holds an apple hugely bitten.
He had not seen this.

Now sees. Squints,
lets it fall onto his face.
Feels the clench of his belly.
The seepage of saliva comes thickly.

Tries to spit, but cannot
force a thing to move, knows he is

hungry.
Eyes widening,
seeing as whole families do
into orange wolf-gleam of the sun,

he feels himself draining too quickly, blackness,
and fire sparks flying over ordinary ground
where all is ash, smoldering.

His wagon looms like one chance
for unity, brittle hope,
one last image

blurred,

near
and just so far.

*for A. G., in memoriam*

## Wildfire

Crackling like fear in the child's heart late awakened,
the parents have gone into nightmare,
on the night lake of darkness
far away are carried, and the house
dreadfully closes.

It smiles like dawn in the wide western window.
No one believes this ever.
But there is glass-flutter.

There is wind hungering and the far sister
of the aspen trying to crawl.

Then it will be seen to leap the ridge distance,
going entirely.
Something has come in the dark, touching.
But the air wonderfully now

is sheepish and light lacquers all.

Snow-light nearly, down,
the singlet of geese travelers,
something like a word from the north,

this wholeness fully breathable
heaping its handful of gray on the ground.
Like mist and fog from a mill town rising
as if the earth had been just
created,

as it has,

and memory's hand opening above the coverlet,
and the family mouth open
and all over.

## Going Home: Ben's Church, Virginia

Packing to move, I unearth something swaddled and heavy,
my grandfather's Winchester pump, Model 12, stock
sheenless and smoothed by a family of hands,
the smell I would know in any dark
of closet or crypt, its great
boom and yellow lick of delight
lashing the canopied undershadow of woods
while morning's blue trickled October dawn.

We sat on the log. Eleven squirrels once. Eleven times
he stood and at noon his bag-coat hung, seams
seeping from small bodies he carried.
Mine then was the .22, short-barreled
clicker, now on my son's wall.
It was as new as I was, sharp-
sighted, never fired,
but right-sized, at any event, for pretending.

At the stream we must cross that cold day he pointed,
then spread his palm on twelve gold cartridges.
Six shots high, the red woodpecker
stoically waited. Then five times
he climbed up the wounded trunk
and turned on me the dark eye that said *no score*. Yet.

■

Going home in his vaulted Hudson, the James River gray
rocking below, I watched oystermen tonging in red
baseball caps, their motions like applause.
Wordless as a log, he stared ahead.
Later, his hands dried, rough,
he held out the pail with pink
chips of flesh rising and falling. And eleven shapes.

"Remember," he said. Did he mean his careful, least
    gestures?
Those gutted entrails that bore blue
shadows amid the bloodied water?
Pumping the breech so it clanged open,
he held the channel for me to look.
From far down the sweet oil rose
like pine sap at autumn's end glazing
the bright hollow, spotting our ancestral stock.

■

At the window, wrapped in grandfather's stained coat, I lift
the family gun and break it open. My son,
eleven, obliviously climbs a tree.
Aiming beyond him toward home,
I remember that woodpecker,
its odd knowledge, the way
it flared with lazy yellow wings
into the dark that spread in my body,
and the lashing smell of the Model 12 in a white
room where old eyes scissored, cut for me, and waited.

# Dream Flight

## Hawaii to Salt Lake City

Mid-January, leaving Honolulu, we are all tanned and strange
    with our secrets tucked away
under seats. Pillows spill from overhead. We lean into them,
    as into clouds, and safely
sail past Pearl Harbor, a submarine and wake clear below


but inexplicable as history or even our mute, cramped
    selves. Over coral and mild miles of
sea dreaming, I wonder how men and women survive and
    explain this world so vastly lavish.
Who are we, so constant in our going down, our rising up,


what news do we cart through the void above the cruising
    unbreakable shadow of our United
hunchback? We feel in its low roar we can climb above all,
    do, and light is shattering.
Many watch movies between worlds, but some glide in
    thought,


in the hiss of space where nothing is known except the
    selves who sit, exiles of speech, humps
of flesh and fear and hope, unable for a long time to alight.
    We see no streetlights, cars, roads,
no hills, no bowl of star-houses to remind us of anyone's life


in the home we dream. Great fish, down there, nose through
    whatever falls on a wind
of water. In their lives there is nothing unremembered or
    known. They go no place in love
or joy. If there is a shadow they enter it and become it

without fear, without knowledge that what they are always
in is themselves, that harmony.
Dreaming of fish, I drift, I imagine the loved ones we fly to,
the car that is waiting, soft
questions from runway to house. They do not want our
secrets

exactly, only what we have bagged and brought back, gifts
for children, what may be kept
from that other, illusory world. Coming home half asleep, I
remember faces I have left,
and left before, their quick eyes in love with whatever rises

out of a place not even dreamed, a word only, like sunlight.
Yet somehow I feel, floating,
I have become a bad gene they already harbor without
knowing. Mid-sea, ungrounded, I see
the plane move backward to start over. Snow smothers the
peaks

of Utah, home valleys dark as the volcano on the big island
of Hawaii where I have not yet
gone. Houses sunk and dormant seem to erupt in the black.
I stand at my child's window,
3 A.M., shadowy as a shark, from homelight about to fly far

over the black bottomland that once was ancient Lake
Bonneville. Newspapers say the Salt Lake is
rising, the airport will go first, floodcrest only one, maybe
two thousand years off. Our
houses will become the spewn gray mist. I feel in my body

bodiless ancestors claw to a rock under star-spillage. I see
        one who is speechless, a woman,
has just buried her children asleep in a mound of wool.
        Silver currents of breath eddy from
faces small by the fire. She squints into the heartquaking

ripple of wind. It makes her eyes water for a man absent,
        loved. Once he lifted her bonnet
by a pond and the sun flamingly poured. She felt herself
        charred. Now she wonders what he has
discovered down there in the salt-dark, blinks, shakes it off,

and tries, expressionlessly, to remember a day she pleased
        him. They breasted the snow. He
roared for delight. The white spume was like clouds. She
        feels unlike all others. Her prayer
when it comes, comes wordless. It flickers from fire, star,

and spruce, from the orange head-crowns of children
        growing fast. It holds the land, unblooming, where
below she will walk, flinging seed from her pocket. Hard
        ground waits unhoused like no-place.
Why, then, do tears glide? Does she feel she has slipped

under the far black plain of air? On the rock she sits ghostly.
        I, too, have stood and sat
in starless air, dizzied. I could not understand the enormous
        roar like selves disembodied.
And once at my child's window heard it, saw a doe's face

swimming toward me in the yard's snow, ice-legged, and I
    felt at my back some houselight
slowly spill into her knowing until she walked it and came
    near and knew me there, all secret.
I put my hand on sealed glass and hand-shadow fell into her


living so it lay upon her one great leap. I went with her, in
    dark. Among fliers head-cradled I
see how a moment of joy looks in and out, always untold,
    always known less than fully by anyone
who stands hard on the earth. But how say such a thing


and not turn the worm that night-long lies in the waiting
    hearts? In time we feel ourselves shaken,
bells ring, we strap our bodies down. We look in the dark
    for the place we must descend to.
So much pressure makes us believe we may not be the
    dreamed ones,


but, more than ever, we are. We remember what we have
    left behind, yet try to think of naming
the little we bring for those we bring ourselves back to. We
    say as we must, everything was just
as dreamed: trees with houses living in their limbs, fish


and fruit to be freely picked, bird song and a horizon
    brilliant as gold snow, a language of song
wonderful as natives whose skins stay honied in the mind,
    and rain pouring like prayer in its wild
surfeit on night-sleep. And from bags will come, like selves

promised, dresses of flowered silk, toys, figures slowly
        honed from the visions of a blind
Chinese father, a hand-carved unleaping deer, a chain of
        sweets, coral, snapshots of the black
self-sealed volcano. These ask no explanation and give none.


They unfold the fullness of themselves, they stand in our
        houses, on shelves, face up under stars.
They warn no one of anything, being dreamless, being only
        what shines in the light of the world,
sent down, as we, into the black ancient lake of air.

## Breech: Birth: Dream

for Dee

**1**
**(Dog, Dreaming)**

*There is always something; and past that something*
*Something else:* Jarrell's words lingering
as late in our house the wild skid of a car
overrides the night's news, snow
icing blind the world. I nod
from room to room, remembering
*all these somethings come to nothing.*

I come to you in your white mound of sleep. My wife,
    before you
there was no weather, no need to stand mouthing
Jarrell like a bitter nut in the haze
where the TV senselessly snarls
in an elder's malignant voice—

in him I hear the dreamed yawning of the world, I feel
how easily the rafters could fly off, the unlocked
night reach down to touch, as I do, the child
lightless in the unmemory of water.
Someone is ready to go head-down
into the sudden scream of self-joy,

                    and I feel the shudder like nothing
else in the world slip up my arm. I look above
where nothing is, into flakes, dwarfed
by a blizzard of lice from the world's
savage hump,
          and the dog lies
between us, brainlessly clicking her teeth,
her long howl, like a snaking river
in moonlight, its path
taking us into time's dream-field

to squat in grass and bite lip
and not cry out, not once,
as the stalks shake
under the enemy's naked feet.

She hunches the floor, the sound of that skull on rock,
the juice of her sex burning at neckstem.
Her flesh pulls taut as a bowstring

as her nails carry her over the floor's field toward us,
you clenched, my hand on your belly, and it comes,
gusting up my arm, the terrible shudder hidden
in you as in a secret of grass.

             At such a moment, almost,
I hear us running, zigzagging low
under leaves already blistered
with blood and dew,
the dream of meat strong in us,
the lure sprung over ground
moon-dazzled like the tip of a spike.


## 2
## (Watching an Aircraft Warning Light)

Then took back my hand,
went to the window, long crusting,
the road vanished, no tracks,

and watched a warning light pulse on a far tower
that, before snow, was near. It was red.
It blurs pink. Or is gone.

How long have I been here, dreaming—

not far now, I knew, from the first hammering light of dawn.
Love had been red on my face as a bruise.

I thought of that red pulsing light: it would loom up in eyes
flying suddenly out of snow,
blinking, then, over wreckage

like love and mercy. Jarrell
was wrong.

*I can feel something pressing on my belly.*
*Is it you?*


## 3
## (The Movement of Water at Night)

Sometimes you think you can remember the world, even
    know
why you lie sleepless while through the earth's body
water crawls against rock and is the dream
you want to enter, the black eddy
you jump into

because the blistering vortex of light on the water makes a
    path
from under your window and climbs onto the bridge
where the water swirls and snaps
like a dreaming dog

and only the heart holds you still. It asks: what is the reason
to be drawn to that drip-drip of nothing?

*Yes, that's my hand. It's me.*
*I can feel the movement, the water too.*

I can feel the face I'm growing at the back of my eyelids.
It's my grandfather's, the coronary's, grinning
down the sheet at the inexplicable
erection, and the tears

fall down my cheeks
to lodge in your hair grayed by snow-spit.
But the light is almost brightening

and I think how, once, I dove too far down in his pond,
    breathless.
I listened to myself clawing up, bubbling
wordlessly not to let go,
oh God, don't let go.
The light boiled.

My grandfather said boy, that's where you come from.
He loved my grandmother. He loved me.
At the end he barked like a dog.
He flooded the bed.

He pulled me from his pond feet first.

I know there must be a way to learn to love
even the incontinent waters of old men
and the bloodstain on sheets,
and maybe those people strapped in
for the Christmas descent
count the minutes
until the secret will be exchanged.

**4**
**(A dream of a Jacklighter)**

Because there are no children in his house, there is nothing
to wake to, crying out.

Because he looks like any father and is not. Imagine him,
long snout of the rifle, a shadow, hunting
at night the image of beauty.

His hand on the cold truck-wheel shakes.
His hands in little convulsions
back-lit by gauges and numbers
that stare at him like love's
unremembering eyes.

Because for a man like him there is nothing else but the
     night
that is beyond the last day.

Because the world arranges such meetings: the deer have
     come,
they stand as if summoned, in grace.
The ice-cobbled road downspools
under his boots, refusing

to sound like a window opening for the burglar. Light
unalterably leaps from his hand and under it
nothing could change this moment
or blot out the sun god

laying breath on their breath. Because they wait, cornered
in the walls of his will, believers
mostly in darkness, mostly
not choosers or chosen,

accompanying one appointed, for whom grass at hooves
    slightly stirs.
Her blue eyes cannot explain him, the shot
rocks her
to buckle under his muzzle.

The fawn would nurse his light except for the throat he
    slits.

Because he must make his dream real in order to remember,
    some things
cry out in absence and some tearlessly wait.
He wants to know which he is.

Because he must violate the world to know
he is in the world.

We lie in the world, unsleeping in fear, his name on our lips
drawn from the steadily poured haze of the television.
This is how he enters each house

silent as a hill of snow, trying to show what has passed
beautifully through his hands.
He would like to lie down between us.

Because someone here is a carrier of truth he cannot bear,
he would take out his knife like a cold wind
we must hunch at.

This is a definition of joy and beauty.
Not what you think.
He is not what you think.

He is only something in a dream we are the meaning of,
    something

to be touched like a deep of water,
a fist of snow
where red dawn comes sailing.


**5**
**(Final Preparations)**

I sit in the room swollen with teary light,
cross-legged like an elder,
willing to try anything.
Is this yoga, and why in hell
do I still shiver?

You keep the crib packaged, the toys stacked
in a closet, not even pictures
grace these blind walls.

*Anything could happen, something. . . .*

The red light I kept dreaming all night
ticks over the clean fields
of our country,
over the long veins of rivers

like the road where this morning
we skidded you in safe.
The phone goes on
ringing like our luck

and nothing has happened,
and I can still smell the bacon
where the water broke at your feet.

I think maybe now I can put things together,
if only the phone will stop,
if only I can think
of something

not the flamed face we labored for,
the appalling livid truth that
love is.

# Two Poems from Western America

**1**
**(A Place in the Forest)**

An opening in thick growth one comes to,
dead-end mostly, trail having declined
without your notice, ideas fallen away,
a thick wall of festering luminousness.
For some the deeply scarred bark
whose flesh-folds hide moss, lifetracks
of the least weasel, a snakeskin.
For others only vines thick-meshed
as family, obligation, that Sunday
when she lifted her hat by the lake.
Even the natural lair of minotaurs.
A darkness hovers beyond, seeping in,
leaves like years are laminated
under foot, and the sun spirals down
an electric chimney of space. How easy
to feel with the same lost conviction
of faith long folded with father's hands,
there is no decision now to be made,
no word to be frightened by. Only *here*,
a gently green wind at the dry lips,
recognized by your body that slowly
is pouring itself like oil down.
After this dream of sitting for years,
there is the casual look for hacked
scars of machete, or perhaps that
runneled and rusted lid of a tin can
once slipped painlessly into your heel
now booted and safe. The needle stung,
you limped for a time. Thinking back,
as if each knoll and root were a clue
unapprehended, the trail seems a dream,
but each step so vivid the least blade

must remember and wait to tell someone
you had come. But what name will be given?
Lying in this space you feel you know
what a great-uncle does day-long
in the whining belly of the Titanic.
It is not unpleasant but very personal,
like a belief. You are sure no one
waits on the wall's other side. No word
exists beyond but will be yours, fully,
as it was once, when you were a child.
You spoke at last, but they had gone
far off in the absence of the house.
There was only your small pink face
speaking into itself, and the word,
shaped to catch the world, only bodiless,
and mother's plants hanging like a wall
about to close on the night-black window.
Now there is the lightless beyond again,
one keeps turning to face it, as if
there will always be one more room
in the world, silent just like this,
as if when you arrive there, alone,
it will be exactly as you have wished,
except empty in the towering light,
the kitchen, voices and smell, not right
under the staircase. But you feel easy,
as if standing at the back porch, as if
shutting the gate, latch not forgotten,
to the alley. Already your body gathers
its spilled oil like an old kerchief
pulled from the air's sly pocket,
a memento from an uncle, close-woven,
useful, unstained, coiling at the throat.

## 2
## (Tide Pools)

At dusk and long-distance they are the mouths
to another world, caves of silence that speak
only in light, and tonight, family packed
for home travel, we take a last, slow route
over sand the sea has been all day cleaning.
At driftwood the children stop, first veering
off wordlessly, and kneel to know some texture
of wood, or stand merely to dream themselves
freely into the gathering shadows of the land.
As we go ahead of them, we imagine their hands
collecting what seems to have waited for each,
shells, starfish, agates like a lover's eyes.
Then we also drift apart, each following deep
runnels the tide has left, and after a while
I see you hunched on a rock, almost a part of it.

The light is nearly gone and the wind chills me
so I think of my father's whistle, how it called
the sundered shadows of a family into the house.
But do not whistle now, through the lips he made,
for somehow we have come where we may be apart
and whole. Instead, I walk farther to the north,
until you are all taken into shapes of this place.

Then I find it, the deepest pool, rock-vaulted,
light bending and alive in water faintly moving.
I see the lacy deceptions, creatures disguised
as rock whose breath flutes in quick freshets.
A killdeer cries from the dark suck of the surf
and, though sweet, that darkness is not wanted.
This hole is filled with the last golden light
and by it I learn to see what I always suspected—

the small, quiet, incessant outcroppings of life.
For a while I stare into the spooling depth, for
here are hard black eyes and iron-shells, glitter
of hulls laid forever side by side like the dead
unwarily caught at last, perfect and untouchable.

When finally I whistle there is almost no light,
but there's enough. You come, then, invisible,
a sound made by the sand, a mingling of laughter,
and I duck under just in time, holding my breath.
How I love your squeal of delight when I burst up
like a king from underground! Soon we are all in,
all naked, splashing and crying like white birds.
The road home will be long and dark, the stars cold,
but collected, like this, we will be buoyed beyond
the dark snags and splinters of what we once were.

# Poetry from Illinois

History Is Your Own Heartbeat
*Michael S. Harper* (1971)

The Foreclosure
*Richard Emil Braun* (1972)

The Scrawny Sonnets and Other
Narratives
*Robert Bagg* (1973)

The Creation Frame
*Phyllis Thompson* (1973)

To All Appearances: Poems New
and Selected
*Josephine Miles* (1974)

Nightmare Begins Responsibility
*Michael S. Harper* (1975)

The Black Hawk Songs
*Michael Borich* (1975)

The Wichita Poems
*Michael Van Walleghen* (1975)

Cumberland Station
*Dave Smith* (1977)

Tracking
*Virginia R. Terris* (1977)

Poems of the Two Worlds
*Frederick Morgan* (1977)

Images of Kin: New and Selected
Poems
*Michael S. Harper* (1977)

On Earth as It Is
*Dan Masterson* (1978)

Riversongs
*Michael Anania* (1978)

Goshawk, Antelope
*Dave Smith* (1979)

Death Mother and Other Poems
*Frederick Morgan* (1979)

Local Men
*James Whitehead* (1979)

Coming to Terms
*Josephine Miles* (1979)

Searching the Drowned Man
*Sydney Lea* (1980)

With Akhmatova at the Black Gates
*Stephen Berg* (1981)

More Trouble with the Obvious
*Michael Van Walleghen* (1981)

Dream Flights
*Dave Smith* (1981)